Beyond Equivalence

CURRENTS
A Short Book Series from Gallaudet University Press

Currents facilitates the timely publication of original, innovative scholarship that fosters discussion and future research. Visit our website for more information and to submit a proposal.

Beyond Equivalence: Reconceptualizing Interpreting Performance Assessment
Elizabeth A. Winston, Robert G. Lee, Christine Monikowski, Rico Peterson, and Laurie Swabey

Available as a Manifold edition at gallaudetupress.manifoldapp.org

Beyond Equivalence

*Reconceptualizing Interpreting
Performance Assessment*

Elizabeth A. Winston, Robert G. Lee,
Christine Monikowski, Rico Peterson,
and Laurie Swabey

Gallaudet University Press
Washington, DC

Gallaudet University Press
gupress.gallaudet.edu

Gallaudet University Press is located on the
traditional territories of Nacotchtank and Piscataway.

© 2023 by Gallaudet University
All rights reserved. Published 2023
Printed in the United States of America

ISBN 978-1-954622-17-3 (paperback)
ISBN 978-1-954622-18-0 (ebook)
ISBN 978-1-954622-19-7 (Manifold)

Chapter 4 is reprinted with permission from B. Winston and L. Swabey. (2011).
Garbage in = garbage out: The importance of source text selection in assessing
interpretations and translations. In *Synergy: Moving forward together, EFSLI 2010
proceedings*. European Forum of Sign Language Interpreters. Copyright 2011 by the
European Forum of Sign Language Interpreters.

Cover description: Against a white background, from the left, blue, green, yellow,
purple, red, and pink wavy lines all converge together at the right. Above the lines, in
large black text is the title, "Beyond Equivalence." Below in smaller black text is the
subtitle, "Reconceptualizing Interpreting Performance Assessment." Under the lines,
in small black text, "Elizabeth A. Winston, Robert G. Lee, Christine Monikowski,
Rico Peterson, Laurie Swabey." At the bottom right of the cover, in bold black text,
"Currents."

Contents

Introduction

There is a longstanding need for valid, reliable measurements of interpreting competence for combinations involving both signed and spoken languages. Although rubrics and checklists are commonly used in both academic and employment settings, a review of available rubrics indicates that many do not focus on interpreting performance per se but rather on vocabulary and language. We argue the need for a shift toward more nuanced and evidence-based conceptualizations of interpreting, communication, and meaning, to improve the development and use of rubrics for assessment in interpreter education, certification, and professional development.

We report here on one facet of the work of the Teaching Interpreter Educators and Mentors (TIEM) Center's Interpreting Assessment Project, in which a team of specialists in the assessment of interpreting performance worked to create valid rubrics for use in measuring proficiency in both signed and spoken language interpreting performance. This volume introduces the Interpreting Performance Assessment Rubric, which can be used to assess both simultaneous and consecutive interpreting performance, in terms of both process and product, in a variety of settings. The rubric encompasses domains and subdomains that have been identified as being fundamental to effective interpreting performance. We outline the descriptors for each domain and their respective scoring scales. Choosing source texts, which is a fundamental part of assessment and evaluation, is also discussed.

1

Reconceptualizing Communication

Just as the interpreter's approach to the work is shaped by their understanding of what interpreting is, how it should be done, and what it should achieve (Janzen, 2013), the educator's approach to evaluation is informed by their conceptualization of the interpreting task and ideal interpreting performance. As human-made artifacts, rubrics are imbued with the understanding of interpreting of those who created them. We thus begin this chapter by briefly discussing the conceptualizations of interpreting, communication, and meaning which inform our approach and are the underlying foundation of the Interpreting Performance Assessment Rubric.

Reconceptualizing Interpreting

Ways of understanding interpreting as a task/activity have evolved over the years. Authors reflecting on these shifts in the last decades of the 20th and first decades of the 21st century, particularly concerning ASL (American Sign Language)/English interpreting, have identified several metaphors[1] that interpreters and educators have employed as frames through which to approach and understand interpreting performance (Janzen & Korpinski, 2005; Wilcox & Shaffer, 2005). One of the most common of these metaphors is that of the interpreter as a "conduit" (cf. Hoza, 2021; Roy, 1999; Wadensjö, 1998) or a "passive and invisible medium through which infor-

---

1. These are commonly referred to as "models" in the literature; however, we avoid that usage here, as they are more appropriately described as metaphors or analogies.

mation passed" (Herring, 2018, p. 98). Nowadays, this metaphor is widely viewed as reductionist, incorrect, and outdated. However, as Wilcox and Shaffer (2005) eloquently argue, the field has not fully moved beyond this conceptualization of interpreting. While we may have moved beyond describing interpreters as conduits, we have not yet left behind the idea that meaning is fixed, that it is an entity which can be conveyed, much as one would convey an object from point A to point B. Such a perspective leads us, as interpreters, interpreter educators, researchers, and language teachers, to misconstrue the concept of meaning and the activity of communication, and therefore, the concept of interpreting other people's communication: As Wilcox and Shaffer (2005, p. 28) put it, "through various iterations of the 'role,' educators have shifted focus from actual 'communication' to political and cultural behaviors of the interpreter."

Although many people continue to conceptualize meaning as static, as something that is packaged and transferred like bits and bytes of data, this is a misrepresentation that ignores the complexity of how meaning is negotiated and constructed through discourse. In any communicative event, meaning is constructed through the lenses of content, intent, and form. Participants in a communicative event must construct their own understanding of a given text, whether signed or spoken, by drawing on their knowledge and experience and making necessary inferences. Chafe (1994, 2001, 2014) describes the processes involved in understanding: One person produces symbols (signs or sounds) that have been associated (by society, as part of a language) with thoughts or concepts; those symbols are then transmitted to others, who associate them with their own thoughts in order to unpack and understand them. The latter part of this process is far from straightforward. Communication, and the achievement of mutual (albeit partial) understanding, is thus a highly complex process. It is only further complicated when interlocutors do not share a common language, and their communicative acts are mediated by an interpreter (Angelelli, 2000; Wilcox & Shaffer, 2005).

In connection with this discussion, it is important to distinguish between the notions of form and meaning. While meaning is shared, co-created, and unique for each participant, form is the packaging—signs, facial expressions, sounds, and/or gestures used with communicative intent—employed by interlocutors to share and coconstruct meaning in interaction. Form, which includes linguistic, pragmatic, and contextual cues, is conveyed to our eyes and ears by light and sound waves, by electronic impulses, by print on paper, and by many and various other means. Such forms provide us with the evidence we use to build our understanding, and those forms can be measured, counted, described, and captured. Meaning, however, cannot be counted or measured. Meaning is, by nature, fluid and different for each person, and influenced by individual filters, experiences, and world knowledge. People use language, gesture, and context to share their ideas and intentions. As participants in interaction, we analyze each of these aspects in our efforts to understand the meaning and intent of others.

Communication is at the heart of our work as interpreters, and, as such, a nuanced understanding and appreciation of communication must be the foundation of our understanding of the interpreting task and our approach to interpreter education. As interpreters, we must embrace the concept that communication is inferential and that language is not simply a conduit for thoughts and ideas. We must develop a deeper understanding of "meaning" and how it is negotiated and constructed through discourse. As educators, we must promulgate the view that interpreting is not simply a conveyance for replacing and substituting static lexical units or grammatical structures between languages. As Janzen (2013, p. 95) reminds us, educators have a fundamental role in shaping learners' understanding of and approach to the work: "How the interpreter educator talks about meaning 'transfer' influences how students of interpretation apprehend the text, work to understand meaning, and recognize their own role in the process." It is therefore incumbent upon us to reflect on and critically examine the conceptualizations of interpreting through which we approach our work, both as interpreters and educators, to avoid contradictions and disconnects that may lead us, albeit unwittingly, to pass on misconceptions to our students.

There is a broad range of factors that might be included in assessment, and more specifically, in the assessment of interpreting. The assessment of meaning-based interpreting performance has a much narrower focus, directly assessing the product (interpretation) and indirectly assessing the process (interpreting decision making). Although some may use simple checklists for assessment, most frequently some type of rubric is developed to evaluate the quality of these two factors in any single assessment. Indeed, a range of such snapshot assessments can be gathered to build a portfolio that reflects not only performance but also reflects the growth of an interpreter's skill and decision-making abilities. Reading this section, it may be helpful to have in mind the interpreting performance rubric used for your specific institution or organization to compare it to the expectations of rubric creation and applications that we discuss.

Regardless of the final form of any assessment tool, as we explore what we assess, we must first establish our expectations of assessment tools: What we expect them to be and do and what we must carefully avoid expecting them to be or do.

Assessments should be:

- valid, which means they must adequately assess the relevant, and only the relevant, aspects of interpreting;

- reliable, ensuring our confidence that results are consistent regardless of the assessor; and

- authentic, appropriately assessing the actual experiences of interpreting.[2]

---

2. Sawyer (2004, p. 13) uses the terms "adequacy," "appropriateness," and "confidence" to describe methodological issues in assessment research—yet, what is assessment but "research" into the competence of an interpreter and the quality of an interpretation? Applying these terms to assessment may be helpful to readers who have been long put off by the terms:

Validity = does the test adequately assess the full realm of interpreting, nothing more and nothing less? Does it focus on interpreting processes and products, and not on language skills?

Confidence = reliability: Do the results give us confidence in the interpreter's process and product? Can we expect that if someone passes, they can interpret? Do all assessors produce similar results?

Further, if we are also educators, they should also:

- measure student success at learning what they need to learn as budding professionals;

- effectively inform our decisions about success in learning and therefore our teaching; and

- provide the type of evidence we need to be able to measure effective learning and effective teaching. (Wiggins & McTighe, 2005, Chapters 7, 8)

Approaches to interpreting performance assessment often cling to outdated, outmoded misconceptions about what interpreting is, what an interpretation is, and how to best assess it. Many of these pitfalls are part and parcel of a larger trap: measuring what is easy to see or hear (Fenwick & Parsons, 2009), rather than what is important and relevant for an effective interpretation and effective interpreting. The various pitfalls and misconceptions about interpreting, and therefore the directions where we need to refocus our assessments and what appropriately needs to be assessed, are briefly summarized in Figure 1 and are further explored in Chapters 2, 3, and 4.

Regardless of the purpose of the assessment, it must be grounded in the fundamental concepts of validity, reliability, and authenticity (e.g., Sawyer's [2004] appropriateness, adequacy, and confidence). The assessment (and those using it) must be able to clearly demonstrate that an assessment does assess what it claims to assess. That is, an interpreting performance assessment must assess concepts/constructs relevant to interpreting (validity), not prerequisites such as basic language fluency, for example. In terms of reliability, it must demonstrate that every person expected to review results responds with similar levels consistently. If the assessment is a national certification test, then extensive evaluation of both validity and reliability must be completed and provided. If it is a classroom test, extensive testing may

Appropriateness = authenticity: Does the test assess the appropriate competencies needed for the context/task? If general, does the text reflect general skills? If medical-specific skills, does it reflect those?

Interpreting Misconceptions	Reconceptualized Focus of Assessments
✗ Meaning is a static thing that can be conveyed	⬆ Effective reconstruction reflects presenters' intents and the audience needs
✗ Language assessment IS interpreting assessment	⬆ Interpreted discourse effectively reflects presenter intent and audiences needs
✗ Rules re: frozen/written/language: grammar, syntax, etc., apply to discourse	⬆ Interpretation reflects interactional and cultural competencies of the participants
✗ Interpretation should be assessed differently based on its direction	⬆ Achievement of participant communication goals, regardless of the source and target languages
✗ Miscue/error analysis is adequate	⬆ Identify effective, as well as ineffective strategies and repertoires

Figure 1. Interpreting misconceptions and facts.

not be possible or necessary. But the teacher and the students should be on the same page about what is being assessed and at what levels.

The History and Evolution of Assessment From Spoken Language Translation to Today

Most of our current practices of assessing interpreting have been handed down via spoken language models that focused initially on translation, were then modified to apply to spoken language interpreting, and eventually, to sign language interpreting. As we understand more and more about meaning-based interpreting assessment, it is important to recall our foundations. Some are essential to our current approaches; others serve to remind us of how we have ourselves evolved. As such, many of the concepts need to be explored for assumptions and principles that (1) may (and may no longer be) supported by current science and state-of-the-art research, and (2) may (or may not) be applicable in time-driven interpreting when compared to translations. Yet, too often, those sources have been integrated and then forgotten. We all would benefit from actively examining the broader world in which our field is situated. It is time we engage in this broader perspective, thus avoiding reinventing the wheel and instead, gaining opportunities to learn and grow.

Many traditional interpreting performance assessments currently in use analyze the lexical, semantic, and grammatical levels of linguistic equivalence achieved in the product, and then determine whether the target translation was "faithful to the source, objective and impartial" (Angelelli & Jacobson, 2009, p. 2). However, linguistic equivalence is rarely relevant in a quality interpretation. What is relevant is achieving the function and purpose of the participants, communication via interpreting. Reviewing the history of a few other perspectives on interpretation quality and range, Angelelli and Jacobson (2009) identify some who emphasize the importance of understanding the functions and purposes of interpreting. Nida's (1964) discussion of dynamic (more aimed at the target audience) and formal (more aimed at the linguistic structure) equivalences is one example. He intertwines the importance of both the content and the form in both the source and target texts. He emphasizes that content and its form are inseparable, and that all content must be considered within the cultural contexts of time, setting, and function of the original work to be translated. Nida calls for a sociolinguistic approach as our most effective choice in addressing quality and adequacy in translation. Although published nearly 60 years ago, Nida's discussion is timely for us today as as we examine issues in signed language interpretation beyond the scope of lexical items, errors, and grammatical correctness. Other examples include Newmark's (1982) communicative/semantic distinctions; Toury's (1995) notions of acceptability (norms of the target culture)/adequacy (norms of the source culture); and the overall idea of Skopos theory (Nord, 1991, 1997)—the purpose of the translation determines that translation's quality.

An interesting and important split in early spoken language discussions is especially enlightening as we explore the evolution to our present-day approaches to assessing of interpreting performance (Sawyer, 2004). This split was between the objectivist linguists' perspective of word equals meaning and the sociolinguists' perspective that focused on interaction. The latter recognized that the spoken word (or written text in translation) did not embody meaning but rather only reflected it (e.g., Seleskovich & Lederer, 1995). This is a distinction we struggle with today, as we see a similar split in performance assessment approaches, where many interpreting assessments conflate words and signs with meaning. Interpretations and interpreting are often assessed in isolation from communication functions and interaction goals. Meanwhile, interpreting researchers interested in interaction continue to explore the goals and activities of interaction, and attempt to integrate linguistics (e.g., discourse analysis) as they can.. Few people in interpreting and interpreting performance assessment have integrated these concepts into effective interpreting assessments.

Another growing perspective that is largely excluded from interpreting assessment is that of cognitive science and cognitive theory in interpreting. As Angelelli and Jacobson (2009) conclude:

> [However,] . . . none of the models of translation quality presented thus far

address the "how to" of effectively and accurately measuring quality. The researcher is left to ponder questions related to how "reader response" can be measured and compared; how to determine the variables that demonstrate whether a translation is acceptable to the target discourse community; or how the "function" of a translation is defined in measurable terms. These are all questions that have not been clearly addressed in the literature. (pp. 2–3)

And, they still need to be sufficiently addressed for us in interpreter education and assessment. Angelelli (2009) moves us closer to these discussions, suggesting the construct of "translation ability" and how we might use rubrics. Interweaving crossdisciplinary ideas considers integrating our understandings of test development, communicative translation (Colina, 2003), Skopos theory (Nord, 1991, 1997), and crosscultural communicative competence theories (Bachman, 1990; Hymes, 1974; Johnson, 2001). We can add to these fields our growing understanding of adult learning and learning-centered educational approaches. Angelelli (2009) reminds us that we are part of a larger field of spoken language interpreting and translation studies. She emphasizes that defining the test construct is the first step in test construction, and she grounds her discussion in the literature. Finally, she offers examples from a rubric that she has developed to assess translation competency that professional associations could use.

We are reminded to think beyond our often limited introductions to the broader field (Angelelli, 2009; Angelelli & Jacobson, 2009; Pöchhacker, 2004; Sawyer, 2004), and to not limit ourselves by adopting the individual theories that one or two researchers have explored without first carefully considering why we are doing so. However, there is no question that their work is invaluable! We owe it to those early researchers, ourselves, and our field to expand and evolve from their seminal work.

Reconceptualizing Assessment of Interpreting Performance
Having explored the implications of our conceptualizations of interpreting for education and performance, in this section we turn our attention to assessment.

Historically, assessment of ASL/spoken English interpreting in the United States has been primarily focused on the identification and analysis of errors ("miscues" in Cokely's [1986] well-known nomenclature), which are generally understood to be deviations from meaning. This approach is problematic since it has tended to view meaning narrowly, as something that is in the text, thus perpetuating "the view that meaning can be discovered and transferred and that deviation from an objectively ideal transfer can be quantified" (Janzen, 2013, p. 104). Assessment approaches that rely on equivalence-based miscue analysis have been described as:

> akin to what a chemist would do when determining the weight of a compound: place a known quantity of weight on one side of a scale, the compound on the other side, and remove or add the compound as necessary to make the scale come into balance. But meaning is not so neat; communication is not chemistry. Meanings across languages cannot be weighed on a balance to determine objective equivalence. (Wilcox & Shaffer, 2005, pp. 44–45)

An additional problematic aspect of assessment rooted in conduit or transference conceptualizations of interpreting is the fact that such approaches are imbued with the assumption that communication is by nature successful—that achieving equivalence of meaning will ensure successful communication. This assumption is a faulty one; in fact, communication is often fraught with partial and/or complete misunderstandings. (e.g., Bazerman, 2014; Chafe, 1994, 2001, 2014; Reddy, 1979, 1993; Tannen, 1986, 1989).

Viewing interpreting through the perspective of conveyance and transference, rather than on the basis of the more nuanced and contextualized conceptualization described in the previous section, has far-reaching implications for the assessment of interpreting, both in terms of process and product. Implicit within a conveyance/transfer view is the assumption that meaning exists as a single, correct, and immutable artifact. This assumption, whether explicit or implicit, leads to approaches to assessment that involve comparing target language product with source language meaning, or that seek to evaluate equivalence (or lack thereof) between the source language and target language texts. Such approaches do not reflect current understandings of the coconstructed nature of communication. As Wilcox and Shaffer (2005, p. 45, emphasis in original) highlight, "we do not have direct access to *the meaning* (as if there is only one!) of the source text, and, if we are third-party evaluators of an interpreted text, neither do we have direct access to *the meaning* of the target text." As evaluators of someone else's performance, we only have access to our individual deconstructed (and reconstructed) understanding of the text.

Assessment-related discourse that refers to determining equivalence between source language and target language suggests, erroneously, that there is only one right way to interpret a given text. It implies that complete equivalence of meaning between a source and target text is achievable, although, in reality, the notion of equivalence is a fuzzy one involving inference, approximation, and compromise (cf. Baker, 2018). Approaches to assessment that view meaning as in the text and that focus primarily on whether or not equivalence was achieved lead evaluators—and interpreters—to mistakenly assess interpretations in a binary fashion: That is, that a given interpretation is good or bad, meaning that, on the one hand, it has achieved equivalence, and, on the other hand, that has not done so.

This type of binary, error-focused approach does not reflect the contextualized nature of communication, and does not allow for nuanced assessment of interpreting performance and product. It also fails to account for the situatedness of communication—as Quinto-Pozos (2013, p. 12) reminds us, "a message is communicated in different ways to people across different situations, and this must be considered when evaluating interpretations"—and for the potential for miscommunication inherent in any attempt at communication.

An additional issue that compounds the problematic nature of assessments focused on miscues and error analysis is that, in the U.S. context, assessment has tended to focus on linguistic issues to the detriment of other aspects of interpreting performance. The scope of analysis is often narrowed in scope, such that the primary focus is on the interpreter's language use, and, more specifically, on individual words, signs, or phrases (and, in many cases, specifically on usage of ASL), rather than on other aspects of interpreting performance and decision making (Smith & Maroney, 2018; Winston, 2023). The tendency to focus on assessing language (and, in particular, ASL) can be traced back to the fact that interpreter education in the United States has often involved teaching language alongside, or even instead of, teaching interpreting. This has led to a lopsided educational program in which the development of "the whole interpreter" (Smith & Maroney, 2018, p. 6) is neglected because of the need to focus on the acquisition and development of language skills in ASL. We argue that assessment of both students and professional interpreters must evaluate interpreting rather than being primarily focused on language, which is only one facet of the interpreting task.

Our approach to assessment must consider more than surface-level linguistic equivalence and draw on our understanding of the coconstructed and situated nature of meaning within a communicative context. As part of this approach, we must move beyond focusing solely on errors and also attend to the (in)effectiveness of the interpretation in context. Such an approach will also take into account "the specifications of the particular translation to be performed and . . . the user's needs" in judging the "adequacy" of the interpreter's performance (Hatim & Mason, 1990, p. 8). Successful communication—whether it is interpreter mediated—should not be taken for granted. Rather, as Bazerman (2014, p. 229) states, "[instead of] taking transparency of language as the norm, we should rather take those situations that achieve high degrees of alignment, shared meaning, and reliability of co-reference as specific accomplishments, to be examined for the special means of achievement in their situation."

Although the users of the interpretation are the final arbiters of the (in) effectiveness of a given interpretation, assessment of the product in consultation with users cannot be our sole form of assessment. In assessing interpreting performance and ability, our focus must encompass both product quality and process—the interpreter's skill and decision making (Angelelli, 2009; Jacobson, 2009; Kim, 2009; Larson, 1984; Nida, 1977; Russell & Malcolm, 2009). Particularly in the context of interpreter education and professional certification, we must have mechanisms to assess the processes that led to the production of the product. Interpreting involves an array of complex processes and decisions, all of which are reflected in the product. Therefore, a complete assessment of interpreting performance requires analysis and evaluation of both process and product and must take into account "the context and facts about shared and unshared knowledge among participants" (Quinto-Pozos, 2013, p. 120).

In moving away from the binary approach to judging equivalence (or lack thereof), we must adopt a holistic, evidence-based approach to assessment, fully appreciating the complexities of communication, coconstruction of meaning, and interpreting performance. Assessment of interpreting performance must be based on research about successful communication with and through interpreters. We need to study the features of a successfully interpreted interaction and then base our assessments on those criteria. Our aim must be to assess effective interpreting practice rather than to identify deviations from an imagined ideal. We must take as our starting point the expectation (norm) that communication success is likely to be partial and that participants' understandings and worldviews are likely to differ—and then focus our assessment on the factors and aspects of the interpreter's work that have contributed to the communicative success, which needs to include the participants' judgments of the interpretation's effectiveness in supporting their (the participants') communication. In doing so, we must point to and analyze moments of success and areas for concern; we must address instances of "meticulous strategizing" (Leeson, 2005) as well as evidence of inadequate processing or decision making. In so doing, we can productively employ terminology such as "(in)effective," "(un)successful," or "(not) functionally accurate" to describe interpreting performance. Rather than discussing achieving equivalence, we might more productively discuss approximating, as closely as possible, the interpreter's best understanding of the source language meaning, taking into account the context/situation, broadly writ, and the people involved in communication. As we pursue the reconceptualizing and refocusing of interpreting assessment, we next review rubrics as the tool we have chosen to frame our project.

2

Rubrics for Assessment

We began our search for an effective and appropriate rubric by reviewing the history of interpreting assessment and the larger context of how this has shaped our broader concepts of assessment in general. There are many ways to approach assessment and evaluation, and usually the more varied, the more complete picture of competence we can form. Types of assessment include knowledge testing and performance testing. Tests of knowledge will use questions such as yes/no; multiple choice; fill in the blanks; and open-ended essays, which are often scored by identifying correct answers rather than reflective responses indicating a deeper analysis of a situation. Performance tests, such as completing a task on the spot or completing various parts of a task at different times, often use checklists and rubrics for scoring. These might range from brief and basic checklists: does the candidate have "it": a bachelor's degree, interpreting certification; to rubrics that score complex traits and performance success. Further, skills and knowledge are often assessed via third-party input, such as experts' observations, supervisors' reports, mentors' feedback, or letters of recommendation.

Finally, all of these can be combined into portfolios, which are collections of competencies demonstrated via various avenues. Russell and Malcolm (2009) provide a comprehensive discussion of the AVLIC certification assessment, sharing an insider's perspective of this interpreting exam. Malcolm (1996) provides a clear and succinct discussion of portfolios used in interpreting education. There are also a variety of more generic rubrics and rubrics development sites that can inform rubric development, including, as a few examples, Assessment Strategies and Tools: Checklists, Rating Scales and Rubrics; RubiStar; and Authentic Assessment Toolbox.1 Most often in performance assessment, some type of rubric is developed to assess the quality level of the performance. Rubrics are intended to take our subjective intuitions about a performance, in this case, an interpretation and/or the interpreting we see, and turn it into a process that is supported by evidence, observations, and objective measures to the extent possible. While no rubric will completely eliminate our intuition and expertise, it can and should help us explain and support our assessments and, in the end, help those being assessed learn and grow through the experience. Further, it can remind us of our biases and ingrained patterns of thought. For example, our own language styles, be they grounded or influenced by race, gender, age, nationality, and/or education, can easily result in us, as educators or as assessors, labeling something as wrong simply because it is not our way of communicating. This can be especially problematic when working with students or interpreters from marginalized linguistic communities. Using rubrics that remind us of the diversity of communication among people in different settings and with differing goals and intentions is a valuable addition to our skill set.

In the following sections, we will discuss the components of rubrics, along with specific interpreting practices. We review some performance assessment approaches and begin to look at specific constructs and features that people use to assess interpreting performance skills. You might find it useful to identify a rubric or checklist that you use or plan to use, or that your institution or agency uses, to explore its construction and practicality for assessing interpreting performance.

---

1. Assessment Strategies and Tools: Checklists, Rating Scales and Rubrics: http://www.learnalberta.ca/content/mewa/html/assessment/checklists.html; RubiStar: http://rubistar.4teachers.org; Authentic Assessment Toolbox: http://jfmueller.faculty.noctrl.edu/toolbox/portfolios.htm

Rubric Components

While performance assessment rubrics can be categorized as either holistic or trait-analytic, it is more useful to consider these as a continuum, where a holistic rubric is more general, and often used in summative evaluations (e.g., certification tests), and trait-analytic rubrics are more specific, and are often used for formative teaching and learning purposes (the differences can be seen in the following rubric discussion). Regardless, every rubric requires three major components: (1) the domains to be assessed, (2) the scale used to assess, and (3) the descriptors that relate the scale to the expected skills in each domain. In addition, any rubric is most effectively used when parameters and specifically defined contexts are provided. These include defining the types of settings and texts where the rubric can be effectively applied, and describing factors that will impact assessment scores. These can include, but are not limited to, describing the purpose of the assessment, the receiver and presenter goals, as well as setting expectations, such as whether and how interpreters are to demonstrate process management (e.g., interruptions, need for clarifications, and indications of challenges in the environment).

Regardless of the level of detail provided, ranging from holistic to trait-analytic, every rubric must have these three components: domains, also referred to as criteria or categories; a scale; and descriptors that relate the scale to the domains (or the domains to the scale). To develop these, either for large-scale, professional-level gatekeeping (e.g., Registry of Interpreters for the Deaf [RID], Educational Interpreting Performance Assessment [EIPA], Board for Evaluation of Interpreters [BEI]) or for daily individualized on-the-spot assessments, rubric measures need to make consistent scoring possible across time and assessors, whether those assessors be certification evaluators, teachers in a program, or mentors working with novice interpreters. The more this is achieved, the more reliable the rubric is considered.

Domains

Domains are the essential elements of whatever skill is being assessed. In our considerations, the domains are the elements that we deem essential for creating an effective interpretation. One important and common sense requirement is that the domains being assessed are actually important to the overall performance, and completely cover the elements required. They are identified by experts based on research and by ongoing comparisons to consumers' needs. If these requirements are met, the assessment is valid—it tests what it claims to test. Unfortunately, in our field, the domains that are often assessed fail to assess interpreting. Instead, the domains of many rubrics in our field focus primarily on assessing basic language skills. While these are certainly easily identified in an interpretation, they are fundamental prerequisites to effective interpreting, and are not interpreting domains in and of themselves. It is indisputable that competence in each of the languages involved is essential. But competence in each language must be established before studying interpreting. Developing and assessing language competencies is not the primary focus of the evaluation of interpreting. Language skills-centered approaches to assessing interpreting skills and competencies at best distract from, and at worst neglect, the assessment of the quality of the interpretation as a whole and do not do justice to the communities that depend on, and expect, effective interpreting in their daily lives.

Recent approaches to assessing interpreting have begun to focus on interpreting criteria. In spoken language interpreting, rubrics developed by Sawyer (2004) and Angelelli (2009) reflect an understanding of this need. Other approaches and analyses have begun to focus more on interpreting and on the ways each language user constructs meaning. Rubrics that focus on how meaning is constructed still include language issues. Still, they focus on how language is used in the source language and guide the reconstruction of similar meanings in the target language. Janzen (2005) explores the many layers of linguistic and cognitive decision making that an interpreter faces all the time. He explores the differences between ASL and English as languages and discusses many of the challenges that these differences bring to interpreting practice, especially if we are approaching it as a meaning-based activity in which we actively coconstruct meaning in our work. Rubrics that describe features, structures, and metastructures that reflect meaning in each language, and compare how they are used, both similarly and differently, assess interpreting performance[2] (e.g., Angelelli, 2009; Sawyer, 2004).

2. It should be noted that some interpreting performance rubrics do include some

Domains need to focus on how the interpretation and the interpreter reconstruct the content, intent, and discourse usages effectively for any given setting. Effective use does entail using appropriate discourse structures in the target. For example, if the source uses constructed dialogue for formal emphasis, the interpreter's choice of appropriate target discourse features for formal emphasis needs to be assessed, rather than their ability to understand constructed dialogue. Each of the domains and subdomains discussed next focus on interpreting interaction using language, rather than on the production and/or comprehension of one language or the other. These are the criteria needed to create a successful interpretation for consumers.[3]

1. Domain: Meaning Reconstruction (i.e., interpretation—the product) **(Weighting = 75%)**

    A.   Subdomain: Content
       ◊ reflects patterns of understanding and reconstruction of the major and minor themes

    B.   Subdomain: Intent/Purposes
       ◊ reflects patterns of understanding and reconstruction of the discourse and interactional intent of the participants (source and/or target)

    C.   Subdomain: Communicative Cues
       ◊ appropriate linguistic and communicative cues (e.g., lexical choices, discourse structures and strategies, contextualization cues) are reconstructed to achieve the intended purposes of the source and/or target participants

2. Domain: Interpreting Performance Repertoires (i.e., the interpreting process) **(Weighting = 15%)**. Interpreter demonstrates skills in and solutions to interpreting processes and challenges, in:

---

language assessment out of necessity based on interpreters' actual language skills. This does not make the inclusion appropriate for assessing interpreting and is often an unavoidable reality. We must consider how our acceptance of this impacts the success of consumers.

3. These are the basic domains and descriptors we propose for a meaning-based interpreting rubric, and are discussed in depth in Chapter 3.

   A.   Subdomain: Content Management
      ◊ clarifying intended purposes and goals (e.g., preparation of materials, educating consumers)
      ◊ monitoring and management of accuracy, participants' goals/purposes (e.g., notes when a mistake is made, information is missed, corrects it, and communicates it to the participants effectively)

   B.   Subdomain: Interaction Management
      ◊ presentation of professional self and alignment (with participants—source and target)
      ◊ speed of presentation, interactions, turn-taking (overlaps, interruptions, backchanneling)

3. Domain: Interpreting Setting Management (**Weighting = 10%**). Interpreter demonstrates creative skills and solutions in managing and maintaining an environment conducive to effective interaction of participants

   A.   Subdomain: Situation/Environmental Management   (e.g., visual and auditory access)

   B.   Subdomain: Ergonomic Management. Interpreter demonstrates self-care (e.g., breaks, position)

The concept of assessing interpreting, rather than language and vocabulary, is an old idea, but for many in signed language interpreting, it is a novel and sometimes challenging concept. Many of the actual features assessed are similar; it is more often the mindset that is challenging. For example, instead of assessing English or ASL vocabulary, the rubric reinforces the shift to assessing how the source content and intent are effectively (or not) interpreted, that is to say, coconstructed, in the target language by the interpreter. This may seem a small point, but as our rubrics often drive and inform feedback, so does our feedback inform and guide interpreters' learning.

Many interpreters and educators today believe, implicitly and explicitly, that assessing language is assessing interpreting and that interpreting is simply a byproduct of language skills. Two commonly used rubrics reflect this approach (whether they reflect the mindset of the developers is not known).

As an analysis of the EIPA (Maroney & Smith, 2010) has only a ~14% focus on interpreting. Following their approach, Winston (2023) analyzed several existing rubrics for their focus on interpreting rather than language. As another example, Taylor's rubrics (2002, 2017) focus on interpreting only ~23% of the entire rubric. They are couched in examples of ineffective interpreting practices, and they offer explicit descriptions to those struggling with what people often label as interpreting when in reality they are struggling with basic language acquisition. These do not effectively measure interpreting performance and may be misleading to users who think they do so.

As noted previously, skills in both languages are critical foundations for interpreting. However, just as being a skilled ASL signer or English speaker does not magically turn a person into a skilled interpreter, assessing ASL and English skills does not magically measure interpreting competence. Any rubric that focuses on the correctness of language structures per se (ASL or English lexical levels, ASL or English prosodic production), levels of articulation (also known as sign production) affect, grammatical structures (ASL verb depiction, English grammar NMS, constructed dialogue, use of space) leads us to assess basic language competencies, and not interpreting. This type of assessment rubric, with such a focus on language rather than on interpreting, exacerbates the trend in interpreter education identified by Maroney and Smith (2010). They note that

> interpreter education has primarily focused on ASL acquisition and competence of second language users. Historically, when interpreting students were not developing requisite ASL skills in short-term programs, programs were made longer and ASL requirements increased. This focus on ASL development neglects the development of the whole interpreter. (p. 6)

Two rubrics currently used in the field of ASL/English interpreting, the EIPA and Taylor's domains (2002, 2017), are briefly discussed here in relation to the expectations of interpreting assessment domains.

EDUCATIONAL INTERPRETER PERFORMANCE ASSESSMENT (EIPA)

As one example, an analysis of the EIPA (Maroney & Smith, 2010; Smith & Maroney 2018), which is a commonly used interpreting assessment, reveals that of the 36 equally weighted "interpreting" criteria listed as being assessed, 69% (25/36) focused on ASL production and fluency. Another 17% (6/36) focused on English production and fluency, and only 14% (5/36) focused on what might be considered actual interpreting skills and processes. Further, the language criteria under both languages focus on basic language competence at the phonology-syntax levels (e.g., use of [sign space] verb directionality/pronominal system; can read and convey signs). The "interpreting" skills criteria include "follows the grammar of ASL or PSE" and "sentence boundaries."

However, a more detailed analysis, still counting only the criteria, shows that of the 25 criteria labeled as ASL, a more accurate/precise label would be "some sort of sign communication" since the EIPA specifically does not assess ASL, but rather any signing (including outdated terms such as "Pidgin Signed English" [PSE], now more accurately labeled "contact signing" by linguists). Likewise, "lag time" is now understood as processing time and not simply the amount of time the interpreter's production lags behind the source's production. In this count, there are only two of the 36 criteria that specify only ASL. These are:

- Voice to Sign (production of signing)
    - ◊ Use of Signing Space: I. Location/relationship using ASL classifier system;
    - ◊ Interpreter Performance: J. Follows grammar of ASL or PSE (if appropriate).
- Sign to Voice: Can read and convey signer's:
    - ◊ A. signs; B. fingerspelling; and D. nonmanual behaviors and *ASL morphology (highlighting/emphasis added).*

Interpreting assessment is not basic language assessment. As such, the criteria for the EIPA are perhaps more focused on assessing language fluency rather than on assessing interpreting.

Taylor (2002, 2017)

Another commonly used rubric to guide interpreting assessment is Taylor (2002, 2017). This evidence-based pair of rubrics identifies a major issue in interpreter education in the United States, which is a serious lack of bilingual skills in both ASL and English. These rubrics, accompanied by examples and descriptions that are very useful for language improvement, and used for identifying and assessing skills in language, are more similar to the rubrics analyzed by Maroney and Smith (2010) for the EIPA. While the EIPA has 36 criteria and Taylor's have only 13, they are remarkably similar in their content and focus on language, especially ASL, rather than interpreting (see Figure 1). Taylor lists eight features relevant to English to ASL interpreting—six are ASL language features, one is composure, appearance, and health, and one is interpreting. There are five major features listed in ASL to English interpreting, but two are also English features (English lexicon and English discourse) while two are relevant to ASL, and one is, again, composure and appearance. Comparing the features and categories of the two, we see that the primary focus of both the EIPA and Taylor's work is on the language features of ASL, with the EIPA assessing 25 ASL features out of 36 total features (69%), and Taylor having nine of 13 (69%). For each, the next highest focus is on the language features of English, with the EIPA having six of 36 (17%) and Taylor having three of 13 (23%). In each, assessment of actual interpreting features is least important, with the EIPA assessing only assessing five interpreting features out of the total of 36 (14%) and Taylor assessing only one of 13 (8%).

Measuring language features, regardless of the language, is easy—we can see, hear, and measure them in isolation from the text as a whole. But interpreting encompasses the text as a whole, as the interpreter reconstructs their own perceptions and understandings of the source. Rather than focusing on the easily notable, we need to refocus on the functions achieved through the use of source language features and reconstructed into functions, structures, and features that achieve the same functions in the target language for the target audience (or for the presenter's target audience—e.g., TV news aimed at the TV station's audience, not a specific group of deaf people). To echo

Rubric Scales for Interpreting Performance

WASLI	Beginning-1	Developing-2	Competent-3	Proficient-4	No level 5	
NIEC IEP Outcomes	Novice presence	Emerging presence	Strong presence	Mature presence	No level 5	
US Ed gov	1	2	3	4	No level 5	
Sawyer 2004, p. 241 or						
GSTI Faculty Handbook (p. 26)	Fail	Borderline fail	Pass	High pass	No level 5	
ATA	Minimal	Deficient	Acceptable	Strong	No level 5	
EIPA	0 1	2	3	4	5	
Taylor	1-N/A	2-Not evident	3-Emerging	4-Inconsistent	5-Consistent	6-Mastered

Rubric Scales for Language Fluency

ASLPI	0 1	2	3	4	5	
SLPI	Novice	Survival	Intermediate	Advanced	Superior	
ACTFL	Novice	None	Intermediate	Advanced	No level 5	

Figure 2. Rubric scales. Note. WASLI = World Association of Sign Language Interpreters; NIEC = National Interpreter Education Center; GSTI = Graduate School of Interpreting and Translation; ATA = American Translators Association; EIPA = Educational Interpreter Performance Assessment; ASLPI = ASL Proficiency Interview; SLPI = Sign Language Procifiency Interview; ACTFL = American Council on the Teaching of Foreign Languages.

Maroney and Smith, it is time to "shift the focus from just ASL development/ competence to include the professional practice of interpreting" (2010).

Scales

Scales can cover different scopes and levels of achievement. They should be contextualized within the profession; the performance levels should be established by the field and consumers and scored accordingly.[4] Scales can range from measuring entry-level proficiency in a field to scales that measure growth and learning over time (e.g., from entry to exit of a preparation program; from the start to the end of a course or workshop). Typically scales have 4 to 5 levels.

Scales for performance assessment rubrics need to be based on observable, consistent, and reliable identified levels of achievement (valid), and rated by each assessor with a similar understanding of their intent (reliable). They are not based on the feelings, likes, or dislikes of a single assessor. They are not Likert scales, although many people confuse these with the Likert scale. A Likert scale is a rating scale, often found on survey forms, which measures how people feel about something. It includes a series of questions that you ask people to answer, with ideally five to seven balanced responses from which people can choose, and often comes "with a neutral midpoint" (downloaded September, 18, 2019, from https://wp-forms.com/beginners-guide-what-is-a-likert-scale-and-how-to-use-it/). Performance assessment scales do not come with a neutral midpoint—they are not intended to measure our feelings about someone, and the scale increments are not intended to offer a set of balanced choices, but a series of ever-more skilled interpreting performances. However, this is rarely explicitly stated and again is often misunderstood, with those less experienced with assessment assuming that the highest level is required. While organizations responsible for assessment can arbitrarily set these scales, they rarely do so explicitly, creating confusion and at times even resentment and widescale loss of credibility by failing to do so.

---

4. It is notable that as a profession, we currently have no standardized, fieldwide scales for language competencies or for entry to interpreting practice. As of 2022, the Conference of Interpreter Trainers (CIT) has been the first organization to develop and discuss any such standards, but they have not been formally adopted.

In Figure 2, scales from various rubrics are shared to demonstrate the range of scales to be found across both spoken and spoken/signed language acquisition and interpreting.

Descriptors

Descriptors are the third essential component of any rubric. These relate the scale to the domains, and indicate the types of skills, knowledge, and/ or performance levels that are expected at each scale increment. They need to offer clear, consistent, and progressive performance descriptions at each scale increment. Effective rubric descriptors need to focus on observable evidence; they should not use language that judges an interpreter's character, value, or worth (e.g., makes *intelligent* decisions; signs *look* nice; consumers *will enjoy* watching; demonstrates a *mature* performance).

It is also important that descriptors offer cohesive increments, adding levels of quality to performance in a domain, not new and different elements. Angelelli (2009) offers an example of consistent, incremental descriptors in Figure 3. The descriptors for the scale are graduated for each domain. The intervals range from consistent and major misunderstandings (lowest skill level = 1), through a flawed understanding (level 2), to a general understanding (level 3), to a complete understanding (level 4), to the highest level of a detailed and nuanced understanding (level 5).

These descriptors demonstrate varying levels of clear, consistent, incremental levels of performance, and focus on the work rather than the interpreter's worth or value. Occasionally, and especially for formative educational purposes, rubric scales, such as the one used in the assessment rubric discussed in the next chapter, may be much more explicitly and discretely detailed. One example of this is the scale for the Interpreting Performance Assessment Rubric (Figure 3), discussed in detail in Chapter 3. The broader ranges between whole numbers are delineated so that smaller increments of skill development and growth can be more easily identified. Also included in this scale are indicators of expectations for professional performance, along with consumer expectations.

1	2	3	4	5
T shows consistent and major misunderstandings of the ST meaning	T contains elements that reflect a flawed understanding of major and/or several minor themes of the ST and/or the manner in which they are presented in the ST. There is evidence of errors in the interpretation that lead to the meaning of the ST not being fully communicated in the T.	T contains elements that reflect a general understanding of the major and most minor themes of the ST and the manner in which they are presented in the ST. There may be evidence of occasional errors in interpretation but the overall meaning of the ST [is] appropriately communicated in the T.	T contains elements that reflect a complete understanding of the major and minor themes of the ST and the manner in which they are presented in the ST. The meaning of the ST is proficiently communicated in the T.	T contains elements that reflect a detailed and nuanced understanding of the major and minor themes of the ST and the manner in which they are presented in the ST. The meaning of the ST is masterfully communicated in the T.

Figure 3. Criterion: Source text meaning. Note. T = translation; TL = target language; ST = source text.

5	Consistent patterns of all skills and abilities are:	5.0: detailed and nuanced; masterful
4 (.1–.9)	Consistent patterns of all skills and abilities range from:	4.8: often nuanced 4.6: sometimes nuanced 4.3: occasionally nuanced 4.0: detailed and able
3 (.1–.9)	Patterns of skills and abilities are demonstrated that range from	3.8: consistently adequately detailed/accurate and able, possibly with rare nuanced segments 3.6: usually adequately detailed/accurate and able 3.3: sometime adequately detailed/accurate and able 3.0: inconsistently detailed/accurate and able
2 (.1–.9)	Patterns of skills and abilities demonstrate that range from:	2.8: often somewhat adequately detailed/accurate and able, possibly with rare adequate segments 2.6: sometimes somewhat detailed/accurate and able 2.3: occasionally somewhat detailed/accurate and able 2.0: rarley detailed/accurate and able
0–1 (.1–.9)	Skills and abilities demonstrated are rare or are not demonstrated	1.5+–.9: rare patterns of skills and abilities are identified 1–1.5: some skills and abilities may appear occasionally, but few patterns are demonstrated 0–0.9: few to no patterns of skills and abilities are demonstrated

Figure 4. Scoring key. *Note.* 5.0 indicates an interpretation that reflects mastery. 4.0–4.9 indicates a consistently reliable/accurate interpretation and effective interpreting process. 3.0–3.9 indicates a fairly reliable interpretation focused on content, and a somewhat effective interpreting process. Consumers should be viligant for accuracy.

Conclusions

One point that becomes clear from a review of all of these and other rubrics available to us is that they seem to appear in isolation, with minimal
explanation of their purposes, applications, and potential uses. Detailed
explanations of the domains and scales are lacking, and most notably, so
are multiple examples of what interpretations produced by interpreters with
various levels of interpreting ability in various contexts look and sound like.
One imperative for assessment is that the assessors be regularly recalibrated
to stay focused on what the rubrics intend rather than straying away from
them. Even the act of determining which level of the scale is appropriate for
various patterns of communication becomes problematic without regular
recalibration. Having worked as reviewers, assessors, and educators of interpreting for many years, we emphasize that regular and frequent discussion
of how and where our assessments align with others and our understanding
of the domains, descriptors, and scales is not only helpful but essential.

Given the noted challenges and our need to focus on meaning- or com-
munication-based interpreting, what does such a rubric look like, and how
do we develop it? Given that assessors still have only the evidence (i.e., the
forms of the product) and no access to the cognitive processes occurring
during the interpreting, we still need to assess what we have and be very
explicit about everything we might assume or infer. For that, it is perhaps
as important to explicitly state what is being implied, and what needs to be
inferred, based on a detailed and explicit description of the context and the
purposes and intents of all participants.

We need a clear specification that identifies the evidence from the source
presenter's language and an understanding of the types of evidence that
might evoke a similar construal of meaning for the target receivers (which
must also be clearly and explicitly detailed). If we include the interpreter in
the mix, as both source and target, we complicate the process even further—
yet we must include the interpreter in this way since the interpreter is both
a receiver and a presenter at every step.

Building on the evolving paradigms we are applying to our understanding of meaning as fluid and dynamic, of communication as flowing, and of

interpreting as active communication among all the participants (presenters, audiences, and interpreters), some educators, researchers, and assessors have begun to construct interpreting assessment rubrics that support these concepts more accurately and effectively (Angelelli, 2009; Jacobson, 2009; Russell & Malcolm, 2009). And in addition, some have begun to develop rubrics that both draw from and support evidence-based teaching, active learning, and criterion-driven source text selection and specification. The meaning-based Interpreting Performance Assessment Rubric was developed as one approach to assessing communication-focused interpreting and interpretations.

3

The Interpreting Performance Assessment Rubric

We have aimed to develop a rubric that views interpreting as situated practice and that takes into account "pragmatic and contextual factors" (Quinto-Pozos, 2013, p. 120), rather than focusing solely or primarily on language
use and equivalence at the word/phrase level. We hope that the rubric will
support an assessment that approaches the text/interaction more globally, as
a whole unit of discourse, and takes into account factors such as the communicative situation, the extent to which the interpretation supports participant aims, and the interpreter's process/decision making. In developing the
rubric, we have kept in mind Angelelli and Jacobson's (2009) observations
related to the difficulty of quality assessment in translation and interpreting:

> none of the models of translation quality presented thus far [in their chap-
> ter] address the "how to" of effectively and accurately measuring quality.
> The researcher is left to ponder questions related to how "reader response"
> can be measured and compared; how to determine the variables that
> demonstrate whether a translation is acceptable to the target discourse
> community; or how the "function" of a translation is defined in measur-
> able terms. These are all questions that have not been clearly addressed in
> the literature. (pp. 2–3)

The rubric (Figure 5) can be used to assess both simultaneous and consecutive interpretations across a variety of settings (e.g., education, community, healthcare). It assumes competence in each language's foundationa

1. Domain Meaning Reconstruction (Interpretation) (Weighting= 75%)	0-1	2	3-3.5	3.6>	4	5
A. Subdomain: Content Assesses patterns of understanding and reconstruction of the major and minor themes						
B. Subdomain: Intent/Purposes Assesses patterns of understanding and reconstruction of the purposes/intent of the participants (source and/or target) 1. Discourse Intent: participant(s)' goal for the content (i.e., inform, involve, influence) 2. Interaction Intent: participant(s)' goal for the interaction (e.g., to offer support; to guide learning)						
C. Subdomain: Communicative Cues Assesses the reconstruction of appropriate linguistic and communicative cues (e.g., lexical choices, discourse structures and strategies, contextualization cues) in order to achieve the intended purposes of the source and/or target audience						
2. Domain: Interpreting Performance Repertoires (Weighting = 15%) Assesses interpreter skills in and solutions to interpreting processes and challenges in:						
A. Subdomain: Content Management 1. Clarifying intended purposes and goals (e.g., preparing material, educating consumers, etc.) 2. Monitoring and management of accuracy, participants' goals/purposes (e.g., notes when a mistake is made, information is missed, corrects it, and communicates it to the participants effectively)						
3. Domain: Interpreting Setting (Weighting = 10%) Assesses interpreter skills and solutions in managing and maintaining an environment conducive to effective interaction of participants						
A. Subdomain: Situation/Environmental Management (e.g., visual and auditory access						
B. Subdomain: Ergonomic Management (self-care; e.g., breaks, position, etc.)						

Figure 5. Interpreting performance rubric—General domains/subdomains. Note. Weighting is suggested and should be adjusted according to source/target texts conditions as well as for consideration of authentic versus simulated performances.

linguistic and interactional skills (English and ASL, or any other language pair). The rubric is intended to cover a range of uses, from a holistic standard to a more detailed breakdown of the components of the holistic standard. The rubric can be adapted to serve a variety of purposes, ranging from formative feedback for educational purposes to diagnostic assessment to summative evaluations of performance.

The rubric is divided into three broad domains, each of which is comprised of two or three subdomains, all of which have been identified as contributing to effective interpreting performance. The domains are as follows:

- Domain 1: Meaning Reconstruction—this is often referred to as "interpreting production" within the field

- Domain 2: Interpreting Performance Repertoires—this is often referred to as the "interpreting process" within the field

- Domain 3: Interpreting Setting Management

The remainder of the chapter describes the rubric and its domains and subdomains. It also introduces the scale and descriptors that accompany it. Our primary focus in the following sections is on discussing the rubric's strengths, refinements, and challenges, as well as on concrete suggestions for use of the rubric.

Domain 1: Meaning Reconstruction

This category, weighted at 75%, assesses the product that we see and/or hear and the effectiveness of the reconstructed message. It replaces what we might traditionally think of as interpreting production. We prefer "meaning reconstruction" as it more precisely describes the object of the assessment. Mentions of assessment of product often refer primarily to assessment of language (vocabulary and grammar) and often minimize assessment of content. Moreover, few if any rubrics focus on the discourse structures that are chosen to reconstruct the source language's goals.

For example, the use of constructed dialogue in formal ASL is intended to emphasize. An effective English target language reconstruction would include parallel/comparable formal English discourse forms of emphasis, which might include pitch, intensity, volume, and pausing, but rarely constructed dialogue. In other words, if the intent of the source/presenter is to emphasize, the assessment of the interpretation must focus on structures that emphasize, not on structures that are the same.

This category is comprised of three subdomains: content, intent, and communicative cues. The labels for these subcategories reflect current understandings of the complexities of discourse, communication, and interpreting. The wording of the domain and subdomain descriptors reminds us that interpreting, and all communication, is about reconstruction, not conveying or transferring, and that our focus is on doing so between languages and people, not within a single language or as an intellectual exercise.

Subdomain: Content

- Assesses patterns of understanding and reconstruction of the major and minor themes

This subdomain focuses on the reconstruction of content. Assessment of this subdomain includes aspects such as omissions, inaccurate additions, and misrepresentations of content, including compression and distortions of ideas and/or links between ideas. It also involves recognizing and affirming effective patterns of content reconstruction. This subdomain is listed separately from those that follow, as the content may be reconstructed accurately even though intent and/or communicative cues may be inaccurate or misrepresented, or the communicative cues used may not be accurate.

Subdomain: Intent/Purposes

- Assesses patterns of understanding and reconstruction of the purposes/intent of the participants (source and/or target)

This subdomain is not usually included as a separate component in rubrics. It is an aspect that can easily be missed by interpreters, particularly novices. It may also be challenging to evaluate, given that doing so requires the evaluator to make inferences or assumptions vis-à-vis each participant's goals and the extent to which the interpreter and the parties (not to mention the assessor) have a shared understanding of said goals. The assessor must also make inferences in terms of assuming or concluding that a given interpreting choice was intended to support a given communicative goal. Nevertheless, we view it as essential. The subdomain takes into account:

- ◊ discourse intent: each participant's (individual) goal(s) in terms of content to be communicated
- ◊ interaction intent: each participant's (individual) goal(s) for the interaction/communicative situation

In the context of a math classroom, for example, the teacher's discourse intent may be to demonstrate the application of a new formula or to introduce student teachers to a new teaching strategy. A presenter's discourse intent might be to engage the audience in considering the ideas by using examples and to persuade them to adopt them. Interactive intent occurs when the teacher provides supportive feedback to student responses ("Yeah, exactly!"; "That's perfect!").

Depending on the type of source text, it is useful to further subdivide this to assess whether the intents of the presenter and the purposes of the receiver are effectively met through the interpreting. This subdomain is also structured to remind users of the full range of complex analysis needed for interpreting and for the assessment of interpreting (Russell & Winston, 2014). Analysis and assessment need to focus on patterns that reflect the interpreter's considerations for these processes and encompass basic and easy-to-identify aspects, in addition to more complex aspects. Envisioned as a continuum, we can think of this subdomain as addressing linguistic issues (basic and easily identified) through interpreting processes, and on through addressing the intents and purposes of both those who are presenting and receiving the message. Figure 6 reflects this continuum.

To illustrate this continuum, an assessment might offer basic comments or consider more complex insights, as in Example 1.

In connection with this subdomain, it is also important to recognize (and take into account in assessment) the fact that individual interlocutors may not have shared goals for a given communicative event—their goals

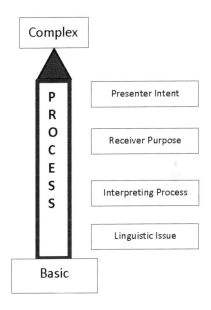

Figure 6. Patterns that reflect goals and intents of participants.

may diverge or be in conflict. Along these same lines, assessors (and interpreters) must be aware of situations in which successful communication is not the goal of one or more interlocutors (e.g., when the intent is to confuse or misdirect).

Subdomain: Communicative Cues
- Assesses the reconstruction of appropriate linguistic and communicative cues (e.g., lexical choices, discourse structures and strategies, contextualization cues) to achieve the intended purposes of the source and/or target audience.

This subdomain is perhaps the most detailed in our development at this stage, with the most possible features and factors. One caveat, however, is

Example 1.

Processes	Examples
Presenter Intent	the presenter intended to distinguish between top-down and bottom-up cohesion—including that in the interpretation is essential by using directional movement with the sign
Receiver Purpose	in this context, the receiver needs to see the illustration of cohesion in the PowerPoint slide as well as the interpretation of the presenter's words—pointing to the slide, then interpreting would help them see the presenter's point
Interpreting Process	the word "cohesion" should have been fingerspelled first, before using that sign
Linguistic Issue	that sign doesn't mean "cohesion"/that is the wrong sign for "cohesion"

that each source text offers only a few of the many options, and what might be assessed in a given situation is primarily dependent on the source text used as a stimulus, along with the defining parameters the interpreter is given before beginning to interpret (Winston & Swabey, 2011).

For the most effective assessment of this subdomain, we recommend creating a detailed discourse analysis of the communicative cues in the source and a similar analysis of the types of target cues predicted in an effective interpretation, with examples reflecting each scoring level.[1] For example, identifying when and where the indirect description in English triggers constructed dialogue or action in ASL, and more specifically, where it might be triggered within the selected source texts, can be both an effective assessment aid and teaching resource. For one example, an English speaker's statement: "Sometimes teachers ask students if they remember something they discussed in the past" would usually be signed in ASL using constructed dialogue.

---

1. Such an analysis is more feasible when using a simulated interpreting setting and text, which allows for detailed preanalysis. However, experienced interpreters and assessors can analyze sources and targets fairly effectively during authentic assessment settings as well.

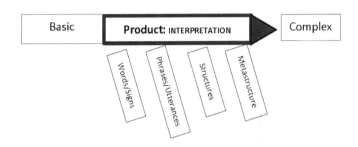

Figure 7. Continuum of discourse complexities.

Currently, many evaluators might see constructed dialogue and evaluate whether it is correctly and clearly produced. This rubric goes beyond that, asking evaluators to consider whether or not the choice to use constructed dialogue is appropriate for reconstructing the English speaker's content and intent. The rubric also provides input about the level of accuracy of reconstructions, ranging from basic (vocabulary, phrases, and utterances) to complex (discourse structures and metastructures, such as openings and closings, topic transitions, and turn-taking). For example, the interpreter might choose constructed dialogue as the appropriate interpreting structure, but still misarticulate it. Assessment of this range of communicative cues can also be envisioned on a continuum, as shown in Figure 7.

To illustrate this continuum, see Example 2 for assessment comments ranging from basic to complex.

At this point, it is important to further consider the point made earlier in Figure 5, that assessment should be the same, regardless of the source language and target language. While this point, in general, holds true, it is also important to recognize that the structures and purposes that are triggered in each direction can be very different. When the interpretation being assessed is an interactive one (involving conversation, for example), it is useful to split

Example 2

Product (Interpretation)	Examples
Metastructure	the formality of the turn-taking interaction ("with all due respect . . . ;" needed to be included to relfect the expectionat of the setting
Structure	ending of subtopic was clearly marked with lowered prosody for the next subtopic
Phrases/Utterances	an English discourse marker like "so then" or "next" was needed when the signer shifted between topics and signed NEXT
Words/Signs	That was the wrong sign for "cohesion"

this subdomain even further into communicative cues triggered when interpreting from one language into the other and vice versa. This further split means that scoring and input can be directed toward the reconstructions from and into each working language. Focusing on contextualization cues that are relevant to those working from English to ASL versus ASL to English makes it easier to identify differences in skills depending on direction and to provide input on those differences. Using a single domain and thus providing a single score for it masks these differences, which are important for learning and growth. We thus recommend that when the stimulus to be interpreted involves two source languages (i.e., in the case of an interaction), raters provide two scores for this subdomain, one for each direction of interpreting. If the source text includes a single language, the split is unnecessary.

Domain 2: Interpreting Performance Repertoires

This is the second major domain of the rubric, weighted at 15%. It assesses interpreters' skills and solutions to interpreting processes and challenges. This domain is more difficult to assess than the first but is both necessary and helpful. It encompasses visible behaviors and invisible cognitive processes, the latter of which the assessor must infer based on what is seen or heard during the interpretation. This domain, as well as the following one, are accompanied by the same caveat as the previously mentioned subdomain of communicative cues. Each aspect of the domain can only be assessed if a specific repertoire is needed, and in many cases, it may not be. For example, if no interruptions or clarifications are required, it is not possible to assess the interpreter's level of skill in performing them.[2] This domain can be assessed in real-time performances and using recorded stimuli. In a real-time setting, the interpreter needs to manage these challenges effectively; when interpreting recorded stimuli, the interpreter needs to indicate clearly when these challenges impact the quality of the interpreting.

Subdomain: Content Management

This subdomain includes two facets:

- clarifying intended purposes and goals—for example, preparation of materials, educating consumers)

- monitoring and management of accuracy, participants' goals/purposes—for example, the interpreter notes when a mistake is made or information is missed, corrects it, and communicates it to the participants effectively

As with communicative cues, this category asks evaluators to leave behind our previous approach, which focused primarily on assessing processing time (or the more outdated notion of assessing "lag time"), counting how long the person waits before starting to interpret. This category requires that we make inferences about the interpreter's processing and decision making based on what we observe in their performance. Careful observation of external (observable) use of control mechanisms during performance can provide valuable insight into the interpreter's processing and self-monitoring (cf. Herring, 2018); assessors can also take note of and evaluate the effectiveness of the control mechanisms employed by the interpreter, within the context at hand, regardless of whether the context is a real-life interpreting

2. While this may seem an obvious point, it is important when providing specifications for any assessment to inform the reviewers about what to do when aspects are not observed. Interpreters should not be expected to manufacture the need for clarification simply because they will be docked points if they do not.

setting or a classroom practice session. This might include observations/ questions such as:

- Does the interpreter ask the signer/speaker to repeat themselves or to slow down, as needed to support effective performance? Or, using video or in a classroom context, does the interpreter pause the video or otherwise act to promote the most effective interpretation?

- When interpreting simultaneously without the possibility of stopping the source language user, does the interpreter inform the target language user if/when the interpreter has missed something, and contextualize or offer information about what was missed?

- When interpreting multiparty interactions, does the interpreter effectively handle turn-taking and/or overlapping talk?

- Does the interpreter effectively and smoothly achieve transparency, such as keeping source language and target language users informed of side conversations (e.g., requests for repetitions or clarification)?

- Does the interpreter take into account the needs of all parties to the communicative activity, or only their own? How is this accomplished?

Careful observations of interpreters' management of the flow of content, as well as monitoring of its completeness/accuracy and responses to issues that arise, can inform raters' evaluations of interpreters' processing, decision making, and ability to manage the situation. These areas also overlap with the previously discussed subdomains of content, intent, and communicative cues, as well as the following subdomain, interaction management.

Subdomain: Interaction Management
This subdomain includes two facets:

- presentation of professional self and alignment—taking into account all parties (and thus all languages) involved in the communicative situation

- speed of presentation, interactions, turn-taking (overlaps, interruptions, backchanneling)

This category overlaps to some extent with content management but focuses the rater's attention more directly on the interpreter's approach to/ management of interaction (rather than on the content of the text, per se). For example, in a given performance, an interpreter may have effectively reconstructed the content but have managed the interactional aspects of doing so in an awkward, clunky, or otherwise ineffective fashion.

This category can be assessed in both live (real-time) performances and interpretations of recorded stimuli; in the latter case, evaluators must inform interpreters of their expectations vis-à-vis this subdomain. The category "presentation of self and alignment" includes instances when an interpreter chooses to introduce themselves (or not), clarifies a mistake or omission, or repeats a missed segment. Interaction management is also assessed when the interpreter pauses (or not) the interaction for clarifications, indicates turn-taking effectively, or manages overlapping speech or signing.

Domain 3: Interpreting Setting Management

This is the final domain of the rubric, weighted at 10%. It focuses on the interpreter's skills in managing and maintaining an environment conducive to effective interaction among participants. It encompasses two subdomains, which are combined for discussion here.

Subdomain: Situation/Environmental Management and Subdomain: Ergonomic Management

The first of these subdomains focuses on issues related to the physical environment, including visual and auditory access. The second focuses on issues related to ergonomics, good work habits, and self-care. These are essential skills; however, depending on the interpreting performances to be evaluated, they may not be triggered or observable in a given performance (cf. Herring, 2018). Individual differences are also likely to come into play—a given aspect of a situation may give rise to the need for management in one situation or for one interpreter but not in another situation or for another interpreter. Assessment of these subdomains must therefore be nuanced and take these caveats into account; it must also consider the relative contextual relevance of the subdomains to a given performance.

Rubric Scale

Scales for performance assessment rubrics need to be based on observable, consistent, and reliable identified levels of achievement. Rubric scales and ratings should not be based on feelings or on a single assessor's likes and dislikes. Scales should eliminate terms that evoke judgments of personality and values such as "good" and "bad." The descriptors developed for the Interpreting Performance Assessment Rubric have been designed in accordance with these best practices. They aim to be descriptive of the product and processes of interpretations and to avoid emotive/judgmental language. They are particularly influenced by spoken language models that reflect these goals (e.g., Angelelli, 2009; Jacobson, 2009; Sawyer, 2004).

In addition, it is fundamentally important for all assessors using a rubric to have a similar understanding of the scale, the categories, and the levels, in order to achieve consistency across raters. Multiple raters using a rubric within an institution or organization must also regularly meet to discuss their understandings of the rubric and of the ratings to avoid drift and to maintain consistency across raters.

The rating scale accompanying the Interpreting Performance Assessment Rubric is based on a traditional 0–5 scale, which can be found on many rubrics. Many rubrics rate based on whole-point or half-point scales (e.g., 2.5, 3, and so on), especially for purposes such as hiring or certification. However, because this rubric is intended for use in education as well as testing and certification, the individual 0–5 ratings have been divided into tenth-point segments (i.e., from 0.1 to 0.9) to allow for more nuanced ratings. These increments allow evaluators to recognize smaller, yet notable, gains over time (for example, while enrolled in a formal educational program). An overview of the ratings appears in Figure 8.

As noted, whole/half number increments can mask evidence of performance improvement over time. For educational purposes, the smaller, tenth-point increments used in this scale are particularly helpful in terms of reflecting areas of strength and areas that need more focus (improvement). Additionally, it is important to understand that the rating scale for this rubric is a performance scale rather than a Likert scale. While Likert scales

	Consistent patterns of all skills and abilities are:	5.0: detailed and nuanced; masterful
5		
4 (.1–.9)	Consistent patterns of all skills and abilities range from:	4.8: often nuanced 4.6: sometimes nuanced 4.3: occasionally nuanced 4.0: detailed and able
3 (.1–.9)	Patterns of skills and abilities are demonstrated that range from	3.8: consistently adequately detailed/accurate and able, possibly with rare nuanced segments 3.6: usually adequately detailed/accurate and able 3.3: sometime adequately detailed/accurate and able 3.0: inconsistently detailed/accurate and able
2 (.1–.9)	Patterns of skills and abilities are demonstrate that range from:	2.8: often somewhat adequately detailed/accurate and able, possibly with rare adequate segments 2.6: sometimes somewhat detailed/accurate and able 2.3: occasionally somewhat detailed/accurate and able 2.0: rarley detailed/accurate and able
0–1 (.1–.9)	Skills and abilities demonstrated are rare or are not demonstrated	1.5+–.9: rare patterns of skills and abilities are identified 1–1.5: some skills and abilities may appear occasionally, but few patterns are demonstrated 0–0.9: few to no patterns of skills and abilities are demonstrated

Figure 8. Scoring key. *Note.* **5.0** indicates an interpretation that reflects mastery. **4.0–4.9** indicates a consistently reliable/accurate interpretation and effective interpreting process. **3.0–3.9** indicates a fairly reliable interpretation focused on content, and a somewhat effective interpreting process. Consumers should be viligant for accuracy. This figure is a dupicate of Figure 4.

Score	0-1.5	1.5+-1.9	2-2.5	2.5-2.9	3-3.5	3.5+-3.9	4-4.5	4.5+-4.8	4.9-5
%	0-35	36-49	50-59	60-64	65-69	70-79	80-89	90-95	95-100
Grade	F	F+	D-	D	D+	C- > C > C+	B	A-	A

Figure 9. Scale aligned with percentages and traditional U.S. grade scheme. Note. The print version of this figure is grayscale, while the Manifold and epub editions are in color.

have an equal increment between each rating level, performance-based scales, like those used in interpreting and language assessments have unequal increments between levels.

Because this rubric is intended for teaching as much, if not more than, for summative certification tests, the performance-based scale corresponds more closely with academic grading in U.S. institutions. Referring to Figure 9, the scoring levels can be compared to the grading levels in many U.S. university courses. On the performance scale, an increase from $0 \rightarrow 1 \rightarrow 2 \rightarrow 3.5$ can be compared to an increase in grades of F (with scores of 0–49%) to D (with scores of 50–64%). Although a student may have completed a significant amount of work, demonstrated growth, and improved by 65%, they are all still performances that fall below the minimally acceptable level. The increments between 3.5–4.0 (65–79%) reflect a growth in skills that approaches a minimally adequate performance of a C/C+, build on the previous 64% of learning, and reflect finer tuning, more depth and detail, and require more critical and analytical skills to achieve/traverse. Similarly, the increment from 4 to 4.5 (B = 80–89%) requires even more fine-tuning, and the distance between 4.5 (B+ = 90–95%) and 5 (A = 95–100%) represents nuanced improvements that may take years to achieve.

While experienced evaluators may understand the differences, for many students and novice practitioners, and perhaps even some new educators and mentors, the whole number points on the scale are often misconstrued as reflecting equal increments on the scale. It is important to be aware that they are not, in fact, even steps when looking at an individual's changes from one assessment to the next. For example, an individual's performance might show an increase of more than 10 points, but where these changes on the scale occur is important. An improvement of 10 points from mid-60% to mid-high 70% might seem large but does not reflect a readiness to work. On the other hand, a relatively small increase of only 2 points from 93% to 95% actually reflects a significant increase and reflects the crossing of a significant threshold. An interpreter who increases from 79% to 80% crosses the threshold for this rubric of "needing supervision" to "able to work independently."

Because this rubric relies on a 0–100 point system, it was easy to convert the scores to percentages and compare them to the grading systems used in most U.S. education systems. In the future, this can make the scoring and understanding of it more familiar for those in the United States who are familiar with these academic scoring levels. In Figure 9, the scale is aligned with both percentages and institutional grades. One addition to this rubric scale is color coding. This proves to be a useful gauge of the correspondence of each level to the overall scale. It serves as a reminder of the scoring mindset for the performance assessment.

Conclusion

Through reviews of assessment constructs and content and discussions with educators, mentors, and students, we have found that many interpreters and educators believe, implicitly and explicitly, that assessing interpreting is assessing language and primarily assessing ASL. Moreover, many believe that interpreting is simply a byproduct of language skills. As discussed previously, this rubric is designed to encourage a move away from such approaches. Although the rubric discussed here does in some ways resemble other existing rubrics, and many of the actual features assessed are similar, the conceptualization of interpreting and assessment—the mindset informing the rubric—has shifted. For example, instead of assessing English or ASL vocabulary, the rubric guides the user to shift to assessing how the interpreter effectively (or ineffectively) deconstructs and reconstructs content, intent, and other aspects of communication, jointly with the participants in the interaction. Experienced educators who use the new rubric may find that such a shift in mindset is challenging.

Although the unintentional and unrecognized use of our ingrained metaphors will require time and patience to eliminate, we need to work to do so. Just as our rubrics often drive and inform feedback, so does our feedback inform and guide interpreters' learning. Shifting from a narrow understanding of communication—as a transfer of meaning based on words and linguistic issues—to a broader and more inclusive focus on all aspects of discourse, including the participants' intents and purposes in communicative acts, is

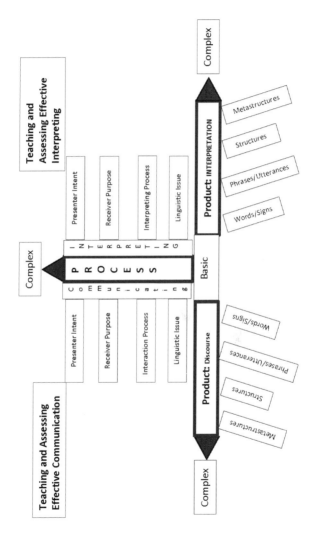

Figure 10. Structures and processes.

essential for all involved in interpreted interactions. Instead of perpetuating the idea that meaning is a static entity and the concept that language is an immutable conduit for conveying meaning, we need to radically reshape our language and eliminate these metaphors from our professional repertoires. It is time to reconceptualize communication as a fluid process involving attempts to share our ideas and thoughts using tools that never completely nor adequately incorporate them. Instead of discussing language and communication as an exchange of tokens resulting in "correct," "full," or "exact" understanding, we need to construe meaning as dynamic and envision communication as a fluid process that is emerging and everchanging, depending on the currents, undercurrents, and observable logjams that we can distinguish in the flow. Our conceptualization of interpreting—and of assessment of interpreting performance—needs to be nuanced and wide-ranging, as reflected in Figure 10. We must embrace this paradigm shift because our understandings and concepts of communication directly impact our work, whether as interpreters, educators, or assessors (Janzen, 2005; Quinto-Pozos, 2013; Wilcox & Shaffer, 2005).

The next stage of the rubric development will be to introduce it and use it in various settings and contexts. We anticipate that this will be an interesting challenge and look forward to confronting it.

4

Contextualizing Assessment

The choice of source stimulus texts is as fundamental to the assessment and evaluation of interpreting as choosing the appropriate evaluation rubrics. Despite this, both informal discussion and interview data collected to date from experienced interpreting educators in the United States indicate that only some can provide solid, evidence-based criteria for that selection. By far the most common rationale for stimulus text choice seems, anecdotally, to be "gut feeling." When pressed, some will expand the rationale to include "authenticity," "good quality sound or video," "length," or "it works." While such factors are important, they do little to enhance a deliberative selection of source stimulus texts, especially in education and evaluation.

The discussion of which source texts will most effectively draw out the kind of interpretation that reflects those features we intend to evaluate is essential to interpreting education and assessment. In ASL/English interpretations, for example, many features heavily weighted in evaluation are found with more or less frequency depending on genre and register in ASL source texts. These include the use of referential and prosodic space, nonmanual signals, fingerspelling, and hand shift. These linguistic features serve specific functions in ASL. Those same functions are served by a variety of linguistic features in English that are often different from those in ASL. For example, ASL combines spatial referencing with lexical items to create cohesion through discourse, often without directly renaming a referent; English requires more frequent renaming of a character to maintain clear referents throughout the discourse. It is the effective use of those features that contribute, in part, to the creation of a successfully coherent, dynamic equivalence in the target production.

The research described here shares the first stages of the input of an international group of interpreting educators and researchers (Winston & Swabey, 2011). Although many participants represent ASL/English interpreting and are from the United States, there are also participants researching and teaching other signed languages as well as spoken languages. The initial findings reported here can be applied to, and be beneficial for, educators and evaluators in considering the source as the starting point for assessing a target interpretation. It includes theoretical and evidence-based practices and practical applications for educators and evaluators.

Project Description
Beginnings
This project is an outgrowth of an earlier project in which several U.S. interpreting educators and researchers attempted to identify the expected interpreting skills outcomes of students graduating from 4-year interpreter education programs. The facilitators of this source text project, Dr. Winston and Dr. Swabey, became interested in source text selection when they realized, after working with the research group for over 2 years, that one major challenge was the result of "gut feeling" source text selection. An initial literature review yielded little information, and they determined to convene a group of leading experts to obtain a variety of perspectives and to identify existing resources.

Convening Experts: An Online Seminar
After identifying those researchers and educators known to have written about, or conducted research in the area of source text selection, the facilitators determined that an online seminar could best involve the worldwide group of experts. The seminar, titled "Source Text Selection for Interpreting Education," ran from June 28 to July 2, 2010, and was hosted in an online, asynchronous setting. The original objectives of the online seminar were to (1) identify existing resources in source text selection in interpreting, (2)

generate questions for further investigation and consider potential directions for future research, and (3) examine current practices in source text selection.

Participants

The facilitators convened a group of 20 international researchers and educators from both signed and spoken language interpreting, inviting them to participate in the 5-day online seminar. Invited participants were asked to commit to logging in twice a day and contributing three or four substantial postings during the conference. As a benefit of participation, each participant had access to the complete online seminar discussions after the seminar ended, through December 31, 2010.

Seminar Structure

The online seminar opened for prereadings on June 28, 2010, with active discussions beginning June 29 and continuing through July 2. Four forums were established, one for posting prereading resources, and three for active discussion. There were a total of 68 postings in the active discussion forums, which were:

- where do we find source texts (48 postings)
- factors in selecting source texts (5 postings)
- source text examples (15 postings)

Although the three discussion forums were established to spark conversation from different perspectives, all three were similar in content, with participants contributing input about choices, sources, rationales, and uses of texts across all of the forums.

Results/Findings of the Group
Importance of Source Text Selection
Two of the three objectives, identifying resources and examining current practices in source text selection, were addressed with some detail; the third, generating ideas for future research, was discussed in a few postings but not pursued in depth.

OBJECTIVE 1: IDENTIFYING RESOURCES

Based on a review of the literature, a few resources were either posted or suggested as potential readings for participants. These included "Assessing Source Material Difficulty for Consecutive Interpreting" (Liu & Chiu, 2009); "Student Competencies in Interpreting" (Roberts, 1992); *Introducing Interpreting Studies* (Pöchhacker, 2004, Chapter 9); and *Fundamental Aspects of Interpreting Education* (Sawyer, 2004, Chapters 4, 8). By the end of the online seminar, more than 30 resources were shared with the group, ranging from articles and informational resources to radio and television broadcasts to personal experiences and specially produced texts. Many of the resources were sites that included a variety of individual source texts, along with tools and materials that supported their use as teaching texts. Participants usually included descriptive explanations about their contributions, describing why a text or source was helpful in their work. The list of resources is being prepared for public posting in the near future. All are being entered into a database that will be available for educators and evaluators to search and utilize.

OBJECTIVE 2: DIRECTIONS FOR FUTURE RESEARCH

Discussion around this objective identified two important directions. Participants described their criteria for source text selection, indicating that they looked for "appropriate" levels of difficulty, relevance, speed, and density in the texts. The need to determine the parameters of "appropriate" in different settings and for various uses was identified. The need for understanding specific test specifications in more depth and for understanding where, when, and how they might be useful in our work was also identified as important for future discussions and research.

OBJECTIVE 3: CURRENT PRACTICES IN SOURCE TEXT SELECTION

Discussion on this topic was rich and broad. The following summary is intended to present some preliminary groupings of the topics rather than a definitive description of the criteria for source text selection. The topic of source text selection as a meaningful focus was an important part of the discussion. Three reasons supporting the need for such discussion and research included minimizing the impact of interrater reliability in evaluation; establishing continuity across teaching practices; and, especially in interpreter education programs, contributing to fairness for students and test-takers.

This objective generated a great deal of in-depth discussion and expanded into two major subtopics, the purposes of source text selection and the features considered in source text selection. Each subtopic is summarized.

Purposes of Source Text Selection
Overall, the group identified two main uses of source texts in interpreting: evaluation and education.

EVALUATION
Source texts, when selected for evaluation purposes, were expected to provide a snapshot of interpreting skills that demonstrated a minimum level of competence for a given domain or environment. Various target groups were identified as needing evaluation. These were the newly graduated student, the certified or credentialed generalist interpreter (e.g., National Accreditation Authority for Translators and Interpreters, RID, AVLIC), and the certified or credentialed specialist interpreter (e.g., conference interpreting, legal interpreting, educational interpreting).

EDUCATION
Source texts, when being used for educational purposes, were selected to provide ongoing practice to encourage growth toward competence, whether for students just learning to interpret or for skilled professionals to enhance skills or enter new specializations. Source texts were expected to produce target interpretations that allowed teachers and students to identify strengths and weaknesses in the interpreting products/processes and could also be used to demonstrate and document growth and progress.

Features of Source Text Selection
Four categories of specific criteria surfaced during the discussions. These were relevance, authenticity, text features, and multipurpose applications. Of these, the first three were similar regardless of evaluation or educational purposes.

The fourth, multipurposing, was discussed in the context of education and simply not addressed in relation to evaluation. It is important to note that these four categories are not intended to be discrete, mutually exclusive groups. Rather, they overlap in many cases. Participants agreed that, in principle, source texts should (1) match or appropriately challenge the interpreter's current level of expertise (for teaching); (2) match the level of expertise deemed essential for working /certification in that arena (for evaluation); and (3) trigger linguistic/discourse features in target language production. Figure 11 illustrates the similarities and differences identified through these discussions.

Relevance

The relevance of a source text to the purpose and target audience surfaced as an essential feature among the participants. Both the content and contextual features of the source text needed to be relevant to user goals/needs for expertise. Areas that were emphasized in this area included:

- Discourse style/type: The source text needs to be of the same or similar types of discourse most often interpreted by the interpreter (e.g., formal presentations for testing conference interpreting skills, medical forms when teaching healthcare interpreting)

- Topic/content: The source text topic and content need to be similar to that which the interpreter will be working in their field or specialization (e.g., medical, diplomatic, academic)

- Number of participants: The source text needs to reflect the kind of interaction that the interpreter is being tested for (e.g., monologue/dialogue)

Authenticity

Authenticity was a second essential category that surfaced through the discussions. Participants emphasized that the use of real-world texts is important, agreeing that texts should be taken from real-world events whenever possible. This does not mean that students and interpreters should only

Figure 11. Similarities and differences of criteria for selecting source texts

practice in real-world events, which could impact the participants negatively. However, real-world recordings are abundantly available now. They can be found in places like training programs for teachers, nurses, doctors, and lawyers; they also have recorded videos for training their students, making them authentic communicative events for an interpreter to practice without negatively impacting the participants. Other sources include the many Rehabilitation Services Administration grant products recorded in classrooms, conferences, interviews, and so forth. Indeed, the internet is full of real-world interactions across many settings and people. It is contingent upon the educator and assessor to identify and analyze those recordings for the traits and factors being taught and assessed in any given course or setting.

However, there was also consensus that simulated authenticity (role plays with authentic participants; rereading of authentic presentations) is sometimes necessary for a variety of reasons. These include meeting students' needs in learning; deleting unusable sections of an authentic text (e.g., too dense, too difficult, off-topic, inaudible); and rendering administration of the text more feasible (e.g., shortening, adding breaks for consecutive practice).

TEXT FEATURES

Text features formed a third category of features that participants identified as important in selecting appropriate source texts. These features are those characteristics intrinsic to the source language that are predicted to trigger specific parallel features in the target interpretation. Not intended to be a comprehensive list, these features included speed, pace, metaphor, idioms, and grammatical structures.

OPPORTUNITIES FOR MULTIPURPOSING

Especially important for those teaching interpreting was the ability/opportunity/potential to use a source text for many purposes throughout a course or curriculum. Some of the purposes identified included:

1. spiraling the text throughout the students' growth and learning
   (translation > consecutive interpreting > simultaneous interpreting)

2. teaching students how to prepare for a topic

3. teaching students how to analyze discourse

4. providing opportunities to compare multiple or parallel versions of similar texts

5. providing authentic tasks (i.e., allowing students to prepare for topics that they will need to eventually interpret)

6. providing practice working with other interpreters

7. practicing selective watching

Conclusion

The online seminar was closed for discussion on Friday, July 2. This report shares a summary of participant input about text selection. Additional products of the seminar were a list of resources and materials for gathering source texts, which are being prepared for public dissemination. Many of these resources were accompanied by commentary from the participants about the various applications and uses the participants found for them, both in testing and teaching. In addition to describing the resources and uses, many participants described their strategies for incorporating them into their teaching. The topic was pursued during a second online seminar, Garbage In = Garbage Out, in March 2011. Participants were presented with a variety of source text videos chosen based on the input discussed in this chapter. They were asked to rate them for potential usefulness and appropriateness for performance testing and teaching of interpreters at various skill levels. It is hoped that the results of these early discussions can be pursued further, expanding the base of knowledge for source text selection in education and assessment.

References

Angelelli, C. (2000). Interpretation as a communicative event: A look through Hymes' lenses. *Meta: journal des traducteurs/Meta: Translators' Journal, 45*(4), 580–592.

Angelelli, C. (2009). Using a rubric to assess translation ability: Defining the construct. In C. Angelelli & H. Jacobson (Eds.), *Testing and assessment in translation and interpreting studies* (pp. 13–49). John Benjamins.

Angelelli, C., & Jacobson, H. (2009). Testing and assessment in translation and interpreting studies: A call for dialogue between research and practice. In C. Angelelli & H. Jacobson (Eds.), *Testing and assessment in translation and interpreting studies* (pp. 1–12). John Benjamins.

Bachman, L. F. (1990). *Fundamental considerations in language testing.* Oxford University Press.

Baker, M. (2018). *In other words: A coursebook on translation* (3rd ed). Routledge.

Bazerman, C. (2014). Genre as social action. In J. P. Gee & M. Handford (Eds.), *Routledge handbook of discourse analysis* (pp. 226–238). Routledge Taylor & Francis Group.

Chafe, W. (1994). *Discourse, consciousness, and time: The flow and displacement of consciousness.* University of Chicago Press.

Chafe, W. (2001). The analysis of discourse flow. In D. Schiffrin, D. Tannen, & H. E. Hamilton (Eds.), *The handbook of discourse analysis* (pp. 673–687). Oxford University Press.

Chafe, W. (2014). From thought to sounds. In J. P. Gee & M. Handford

(Eds.), *Routledge handbook of discourse analysis* (pp. 356–368). Routledge Taylor & Francis Group.

Colina, S. (2003). Towards an empirically-based translation pedagogy. In B. J. Baer & Baer, G. S. Koby (Eds.), *Beyond the ivory tower: Rethinking translation pedagogy* (pp. 29–59). John Benjamins.

Fenwick, T., & Parsons, J. (2009). *Art of evaluation: A resource for educators and trainers* (2nd ed.). Thompson Educational Publishing.

Hatim, B., & Mason, I. (1990). *Discourse and the translator.* Longman.

Herring, R. E. (2018). *"I could only think about what I was doing, and that was a lot to think about": Online self-regulation in dialogue interpreting.* [Doctoral dissertation, University of Geneva, Switzerland]. Archive ouverte UNIGE. https://archive-ouverte.unige.ch/unige:108626

Hoza, J. (2021). *Team interpreting as collaboration and interdependence: A return to a community approach* (2nd ed). RID Press.

Hymes, D. (1974). *Foundations in sociolinguistics.* University of Pennsylvania Press.

Jacobson, H. E. (2009). Moving beyond words in assessing mediated interaction. In C. Angelelli & H. Jacobson (Eds.), *Testing and assessment in translation and interpreting* (pp. 49–70). John Benjamins.

Janzen, T. (2005). Introduction to the theory and practice of signed language interpreting. In T. Janzen (Ed.), *Topics in signed language interpreting: Theory and rractice* (pp. 3–26). John Benjamins.

Janzen, T. (2013). The impact of linguistic theory on interpretation research methodology. In E. A. Winston & C. Monikowski (Eds.), *Evolving paradigms in interpreter education* (pp. 87–118). Gallaudet University Press.

Janzen, T., & Korpinski, D. (2005). Ethics and professionalism in interpreting. In T. Janzen (Ed.), *Topics in signed language interpreting: Theory and practice* (pp. 165–199). John Benjamins.

Johnson, D. I. (2001). An investigation of the relationship between student learning style and oral communication competence (Publication No. 1408979). [Doctoral dissertation, West Virginia University]. ProQues

Chafe, W. (2014). From thought to sounds. In J. P. Gee & M. Handford

Chafe, W. (2014). From thought to sounds. In J. P. Gee & M. Handford (Eds.), *Routledge handbook of discourse analysis* (pp. 356–368). Routledge Taylor & Francis Group.

Cokely, D. (1986). Effects of lag time on interpreter errors. *Sign Language Studies 53.*

Colina, S. (2003). Towards an empirically-based translation pedagogy. In B. J. Baer & G. S. Koby (Eds.), *Beyond the ivory tower: Rethinking translation pedagogy* (pp. 29–59). John Benjamins.

Fenwick, T., & Parsons, J. (2009). *Art of evaluation: A resource for educators and trainers* (2nd ed.). Thompson Educational Publishing.

Hatim, B., & Mason, I. (1990). *Discourse and the translator.* Longman.

Herring, R. E. (2018). *"I could only think about what I was doing, and that was a lot to think about": Online self-regulation in dialogue interpreting.* [Doctoral dissertation, University of Geneva, Switzerland]. Archive ouverte UNIGE. https://archive-ouverte.unige.ch/unige:108626

Hoza, J. (2021). *Team interpreting as collaboration and interdependence: A return to a community approach* (2nd ed). RID Press.

Hymes, D. (1974). *Foundations in sociolinguistics.* University of Pennsylvania Press.

Jacobson, H. E. (2009). Moving beyond words in assessing mediated interaction. In C. Angelelli & H. Jacobson (Eds.), *Testing and assessment in translation and interpreting studies* (pp. 49–70). John Benjamins.

Janzen, T. (2005). Introduction to the theory and practice of signed language interpreting. In T. Janzen (Ed.), *Topics in signed language interpreting: Theory and rractice* (pp. 3–26). John Benjamins.

Janzen, T. (2013). The impact of linguistic theory on interpretation research methodology. In E. A. Winston & C. Monikowski (Eds.), *Evolving paradigms in interpreter education* (pp. 87–118). Gallaudet University Press.

Janzen, T., & Korpinski, D. (2005). Ethics and professionalism in interpreting. In T. Janzen (Ed.), *Topics in signed language interpreting: Theory and practice* (pp. 165–199). John Benjamins.

Johnson, D. I. (2001). *An investigation of the relationship between student learning style and oral communication competence* (Publication No.

1408979). [Doctoral dissertation, West Virginia University]. ProQuest Dissertations and Theses Global.

Kim, M. (2009). Meaning-oriented assessment of translations. In C. Angelelli & H. Jacobson (Eds.), *Testing and assessment in translation and interpreting* (pp. 123–158). John Benjamins.

Larson, M. (1984). *Meaning-based translation: A guide to cross-language equivalence.* University Press of America.

Leeson, L. (2005). Making the effort in simultaneous interpreting: Some considerations for signed language interpreters. In T. Janzen (Ed.), *Topics in signed language interpretation: Theory and practice* (pp. 51–68). John Benjamins.

Liu, M., & Chiu, Y.-H. (2009). Assessing source material difficulty for consecutive interpreting. *Interpreting, 11*(2), 244–266.

Malcolm, K. (1996). Assessing exit competencies: A portfolio approach. In D. Jones (Ed.), *Assessing our work: Assessing our worth* (pp. 47–60). Conference of Interpreter Trainers.

Maroney, E., & Smith, A. R. (2010). Defining the nature of the "gap" between interpreter education, certification and readiness-to-work: A research study of bachelor's degree graduates. *RID VIEWS, 27*(4), 35–37.

Newmark, P. (1982). A further note on communicative and semantic translation. *Babel, 28*(1), 18–20.

Nida, E. A. (1964). *Toward a science of translating.* E. J. Brill.

Nida, E. A. (1977). The nature of dynamic equivalence in translating. *Babel, 23*(3), 99–103.

Nord, C. (1991). Skopos, loyalty and translation conventions. *Target, 3,* 91–109. http://dx.doi.org/10.1075/target.3.1.06nor

Nord, C. (1997). *Translation as a purposeful activity, functionalist approaches explained.* St. Jerome Publishing.

Pöchhacker, F. (2004). *Introducing interpreting studies.* Routledge.

Quinto-Pozos, D. (2013). Making language theory explicit. In E. A. Winston & C. Monikowski (Eds.), *Evolving paradigms in interpreter education* (pp. 119–123). Gallaudet University Press.

Reddy, M. (1979). The conduit metaphor: A case of frame conflict in our language about language. In A. Ortony (Ed.), *Metaphor and thought* (pp. 284–324). Cambridge University Press.

Reddy, M. (1993). The conduit metaphor: A case of frame conflict in our language about language. In A. Ortony (Ed.), *Metaphor and thought* (2nd ed., pp. 164–201). Cambridge University Press.

Roberts, R. (1992). Student competencies in interpreting: Defining, teaching, and evaluating. In E. A. Winston (Ed.), *Student competencies: Defining, teaching, and learning.* Conference of Interpreter Trainers.

Roy, C. (1999). *Interpreting as a discourse process.* Oxford University Press.

Russell, D., & Malcolm, K. (2009). Assessing ASL-English interpreters: The Canadian model of national certification. In C. Angelelli & H. Jacobson (Eds.), *Testing and assessment in translation and interpreting* (pp. 331–376). John Benjamins.

Russell, D., & Winston, E. (2014). TAPping into the interpreting process: Using participant reports to inform the interpreting process in educational settings. *Translation & Interpreting, 6*(1), 102–127.

Sawyer, D. (2004). *Fundamental aspects of interpreter education.* John Benjamins.

Seleskovitch, D., & Lederer, M. (1995). *A systematic approach to teaching interpretation* (J. Harmer, Trans.). Registry of Interpreters for the Deaf.

Smith, A. R., & Maroney, E. M. (2018). Revisiting: Defining the nature of the "gap" between interpreter education, certification and readiness-to-work. *RID VIEWS, 35*(1), 15, 31–34.

Tannen, D. (1986). *That's not what I meant: How conversational style makes or breaks your relations with others.* William Morrow.

Tannen, D. (1989). *Talking voices: Repetition, dialogue, and imagery in conversational discourse.* Cambridge University Press.

Taylor, M. M. (2002). *Interpretation skills: American Sign Language to English.* Interpreting Consolidated.

Taylor, M. M. (2017). *Interpretation skills: English to American Sign Language* (2nd ed.). Interpreting Consolidated.

Toury, G. (1995). *Descriptive translation studies and beyond.* John Benjamins. https://doi.org/10.1075/btl.4

Wadensjö, C. (1998). *Interpreting as interaction.* Routledge.

Wiggins, G., & McTighe, J. (2005). *Understanding by design* (2nd ed.). Association for Supervision and Curriculum Development.

Wilcox, S., & Shaffer, B. (2005). Towards a cognitive model of interpreting. In T. Janzen (Ed.), *Topics in signed language interpreting: Theory and practice* (pp. 27–50). John Benjamins.

Winston, B., & Swabey, L. (2011). Garbage in = garbage out: the importance of source text selection in assessing interpretations and translations. In *Synergy: Moving forward together, EFSLI 2010 proceedings.* European Forum of Sign Language Interpreters.

Winston, E. A. (2023). *Discourse analysis: Context, cues and communication strategies: A practical application of discourse analysis for interpreting.* [Manuscript in preparation]. TIEM Center.

About the Authors

Elizabeth A. Winston

betsywinston@TIEMCenter.org

Betsy Winston directs the Teaching Interpreting Educators and Mentors (TIEM) Center, a Center focused on excellence and integrity in interpreter and mentor education and research. Her expertise includes teaching and research in curriculum development, assessment and evaluation, discourse analysis, interpreting skills development, educational interpreting, multimedia applications in ASL research and teaching, and teaching at a distance. She has been honored by CIT and RID in 2000 with the Mary Stotler Award, for her contributions to the field of Interpreter Education; in 2016, she received the Outstanding Service to Interpreting award from NAD, as a member of the RID Certification Committee.

Robert G. Lee

robertglee@mac.com

Robert G. Lee has been interpreting, teaching and researching for more than 30 years. He is currently an associate academic specialist in the ASL and Interpreting Education Program at Northeastern University in Boston, Massachusetts. Previously, he was senior lecturer and course leader of the MA and Postgraduate Diploma in British Sign Language/English Interpreting at the University of Central Lancashire (UK). He has presented at conferences and workshops for spoken and signed language interpreters in North and South America and across Europe. In addition to other publications, Robert coedited (with Betsy Winston) the RID Press book, *Mentorship in Sign Language Interpreting* and coauthored (with Peter Llewellyn-Jones) the SLI Press book *Redefining the Role of the Community Interpreter: The Concept of Role-Space.*

Christine Monikowsi

c.monikowski@gmail.com

Christine Monikowski's published works include *Evolving Paradigms in Interpreter Education* coedited with Elizabeth Winston (Gallaudet University Press, 2013) and *Service Learning in Interpreting Education* coauthored with Rico Peterson (Oxford University Press, 2005). Her most recent volume is titled *Conversations With Interpreter Educators: Best Practices* (Gallaudet University Press, 2017). In 2013, Dr. Monikowski was Fulbright Specialist (under the auspices of the U.S. Department of State) in Australia at the University of Newcastle's Royal Institute for Deaf Blind Children/Renwick. In the spring of 2016 she was a Short-Term Research Fellow at Trinity College Dublin. In December 2017, Professor Monikowski retired from her position in higher education and now lives in New Mexico. She has become an avid pickleball player and enjoys exploring the Southwest with her husband.

Rico Peterson

rxpnss@rit.edu

Rico Peterson is a professor at Rochester Institute of Technology. An interpreter since 1973 and teacher of interpreting since 1985, Dr. Peterson has advised and consulted with developing interpreting programs in Thailand, the Philippines, and Japan. His publications include *The Unlearning Curve: Learning to Learn American Sign Language* (Sign Media, Inc.) and coauthorship of *ASL at Work* (DawnSignPress.) He was a coeditor of *Interpreting and Interpreter Education: Directions for Research and Practice* (Oxford University Press) and has published in volumes from John Benjamins, ACTFL, the *Journal of Deaf Studies and Deaf Education,* the *CALICO Journal, Studies in Second Language Acquisition,* and Gallaudet University Press.

Laurie Swabey

laswabey@stkate.edu

Laurie Swabey is Professor of Interpreting at St. Catherine University and Director of the CATIE Center. Publications include coedited volumes *Advances in Interpreting Research* (John Benjamins) and *Educating Healthcare Interpreters* (Gallaudet University Press) and several book chapters. She has published in *Interpreting: International Journal of Research and Practice, Translation and Interpreting Studies, Journal of Healthcare Quality, Journal of Interpreting,* and *International Journal of Interpreter Education.* She has served as a member of the advisory board for the National Council on Interpreting in Healthcare (NCIHC) and the CCHI (Certification Commission for Healthcare Interpreters).